101 Ways to Find a Husband

by Maryam Piper

assisted by John Piper and Lisa Stanland

Published in 2017 by
Maryam Piper
Find A Husband
www.findahusband.info
maryam@findahusband.info

Thanks to Catriona who inspired this book by saying, “I don’t know what she wants, but I want a husband.”

We hope this book helps.

INTRODUCTION

The "secret" to finding a husband is to meet the "right" man. The secret to finding an ideal husband is to go about it in the right way. This applies to all relationships, and to get it right you may need to kiss a lot of frogs before you find your prince.

After a particularly painful split from a significant-other, I went on a bit of a rampage and dated many potential partners in a relatively short period of time. Once there were five in a week. While doing this, I discovered a specific ratio was holding true, and this ratio was one in five (1:5). For every five men I met, only one of them had what it took to get me interested.

Of course this also worked the other way around. So only one in five of the men I met found I had what they wanted. Combine the chemistry of 1:5 and 1:5 and the result is 1:25. In other words for every 25 people I met there would be a match.

This is not to say that all the other dates were not enjoyable, or that I did not see some of them a second or third time. But one out of every 25 worked on a much more significant level.

Now a word of warning. This book is not "politically correct" – I prefer to tell it like it is, with no regard for who may be offended. Political correctness is just another way of saying, let's tell lies! I am not prepared to do that because I would not be giving you full value.

I want the people who read this book to get real value and to go out there and achieve all their dreams.

I certainly have no wish to upset you, and if I do upset you by saying something I believe to be the truth but you disagree with or would prefer not to accept, then I can only suggest you examine your feelings and see what you can do to ensure this issue does not upset you in the future!

In this book I am giving you 101 ways to find a husband. Some may seem obvious, but the obvious can be a great place to start. Let's begin.

Number ONE
Meet as many men as possible who meet your criteria.

I'm not suggesting changing your criteria. As long as you know what turns you on and accept it for a fact, then the world truly is your oyster. Of course there may be practical limitations if your criteria are particularly demanding, but that's your call.

How many men you meet is entirely up to you and your schedule. As I said, I could meet up to five potential partners in one week, but that was exceptional. But I think two or three candidates is an entirely reasonable number.

There is no harm in dating more than one man at a time until you find the one you want to get serious with.

Number TWO
Sign up to as many dating web sites as appeal to you

But be careful because some of them are simply scams. I have personal experience of Tinder and The Times-on-line (in the UK) and can recommend both of these.

Certainly you will meet men who may not have marriage in mind, but that is something I imagine you already know how to deal with.

Don't let that sort of issue worry you and be prepared to expect the occasional awkward or downright disastrous date. In practice, I found these very few and far between – even though I have fairly high standards.

Number THREE
Join groups that interest you

Again this depends on your own criteria but here are a few ideas.

Your local gym is a great place to meet fine specimens of either sex, and you get fitter whilst you do it! The same goes for the pool and the jogging circuit. Then there are classes and groups for yoga, Pilates, tai chi and so on. And if you're coming from the other end of the fitness spectrum there's always weight-watchers. As for the opportunities provided by more sedate recreational activities, there are chess clubs, card schools, reading groups, pub quiz teams, even the local neighbourhood watch.

And if your criteria for the ideal husband involves sharing the same values and beliefs, then check out the prospects that belong to your local religious group, or political party, anything and everything that you have an affinity with from the local food bank to the local chapter of the Hell's Angels.

Number FOUR
Raffle Yourself in the Local Paper

These 101 Ways To Find A Husband is an eclectic list, and I make no apologies for the order in which they appear. So, why not sell yourself, literally! Just for a date mind, with proceeds going to charity. You are pretty much bound to find a local newspaper or bulletin board who will be happy to promote this and you!

Of course this sort of bold approach may only suit the extraverts among us, but even if we are shy we can use that to our advantage and state as much in our self-publicity. It's probably best to start with the charity, and once they have endorsed the idea you can approach the newspaper, or radio station, or crowd-funding site, or even a suitable TV channel.

Number FIVE
Exploit advertising in the personal columns

I have done this a few times and I have indeed met a few interesting people. One ad I ran was very succinct and completely honest. It said, "Perfect Man Wanted." I was highly amused by some of the guys who replied, and it taught me an interesting lesson: it's not really what we are, but what we think we are that is important.

On this score, a girl friend of mine confided in me that she was with a man who asked her to have a boob job. She replied, "Oh Darling, of course I will. But you go first. You know I love you, but you are a little small where it counts!" Yeah, I know it's an old joke, but it was a new one for her to tell me.

Number SIX
Don't refuse any invitations

If you genuinely want to meet new men then it's no good languishing at home by yourself. Get out there and mingle. OK, sometimes you may feel tired and wretched, but that might be the very night you meet Mr. Right. And a word of advice about exes. Trying to rekindle something that has been lost with an ex-partner is rarely a good idea. He is an ex for a reason, so remember the reason before remembering the good times.

Of course you should always use your common sense. If you get an invitation from someone old or new who strikes you as creepy, or bonkers, or simply that you take an instant dislike to, then quit. And if you ever do feel desperate to cut and run, then presetting your phone to ring after 15 minutes is a great way to pretend you've been called away urgently.

Number SEVEN
Encourage your friends to set up blind dates

Some friends are only too keen to do this but often totally misjudge compatibility issues. Nevertheless it's a valid way to meet people, and friends do get it right sometimes. Plus the man in the frame may not be ideal, but one of his friends might be!

Number EIGHT
Start a Business

This may seem rather extreme if you are trying to find a husband, but consider these points:

- Business can be very part time.
- With the right business, meeting men is part of the deal.
- It can be much easier to initiate a business discussion than a romantic discussion.
- Some businesses do not involve any financial risk but can still bring in financial rewards.
- Many businesses involve a constant stream of prospects, like a coffee shop.

You could even start your own local dating agency! It need not have any intention of making money, but it's a great excuse for exploiting the adverts yourself.

Another idea would be to become a supplier of goods and services that the type of husband you're seeking is likely to buy – fitness supplements, antique porcelain, tattoos, fine wines, art house movies, whatever.

Number NINE
Always be alert.

Yes, I know. This should be top of the list, but I told you this book is eclectic. Anyway, always be on the lookout, you never know who might cross your path. Anywhere, everywhere: on the train, in the coffee line, at the game, at the airport check-in, at the supermarket check-out. And when you do spot a man who interests you, try a smile and say "hello."

Number TEN
Get a dog

Dogs are a guy-magnet. A man will usually talk to your dog long before he talks to you, and he's certainly more likely to stroke it, play with it and learn its name long before he does any of those things for you. And you can tell so much about a man depending on the type of dog he's attracted to.

Hey, dogs are great anyway. Specially if you fail to find the ideal husband for a while.

Number ELEVEN
Target your man (or men)

This approach has been tried and tested over the millennia. Load up your arsenal, set your sites, and move in.

We all know most men are generally more delighted and desperate to meet us women than the other way around!

Having said that, you don’t want to be wasting your time on a lost cause, so it's better to target a few men if your prime target proves impossible.

And don’t get arrested as a stalker!

Number TWELVE
Be at your best

I don't mean you should always be perfectly groomed. Being at your best is really an attitude of mind. Stay bright and breezy. Stay fit. Running is a good test, if you can run that is. But it doesn't matter if your running days are over, or never were, and it doesn't matter what weight you may be, it's a question of making the most of yourself.

A positive attitude goes a long way. So stay confident and this will increase your chances. As for what you say and the way you say it, well maybe you should not tell the truth if it might offend some one, but pretty much anything you say may offend some one out there!

Number THIRTEEN
Be honest

OK, we all embellish our details a little, I know I do, but don’t go too far. My husband - yes, I have found Mr. Right, of course I have - my husband is in marketing, and whilst it is important to land the sale it is also important to leave something aside so the customer is not disappointed when they take delivery. And yes, you must sell yourself, but do not oversell!

Here's a story about why I chose my husband. I was on Tinder and getting loads of hits and, of course, 90% were only after one thing. I blocked anyone who wanted “personal” photos, which trimmed the numbers way down. Anyway, one day, before I had even met my husband in person, I was telling him how much I missed him, which was the truth. And he replied, “how the hell can you miss me, we have not even met yet.”

I knew then he was an honest man and the one for me. We were married six months later!

My logic is not to be part of the herd, and mouth meaningless platitudes. Be your own woman, be honest to him, and most importantly be honest to yourself.

Number FOURTEEN
Don’t waste too much time in CyberSpace

You should be aware that human discussion has little to do with words.

In fact there is a rule, the “55-38-7” rule. This states that communication is:

55% body language and facial expressions

38% tone of voice and inflection

7% the words we use.

Now these percentages are NOT fixed and they vary depending on the situation, and also whether there is congruence between the words and the other factors.

But if you are stuck in cyberspace, using messaging or emails to communicate with someone, you miss out on 93% of the information you would normally use to decide whether or not you really like them. In other words you may well be wasting a lot of your time.

So get out of cyberspace as soon as possible and at least talk on the phone, which introduces the tone and sound of the voice, and the inflection. Video communication like Skype or Whatsapp can be another step forward, but our liking for someone is also linked to smell, hence the amount of money we all spend on perfume, and the amount of time we spend washing ourselves.

In fact when we actually meet somebody in the flesh, our bodies and brains assess a mass of information subconsciously to do with their merits as a mate and, as we all know, there is no substitute for a meeting.

Cyberspace is often worse than useless, so get into the real world as soon as is practical. Plus be wary of those who are very reluctant to take that step.

Number FIFTEEN
Ask the universe for your soulmate

This is actually what my husband did. He tells me I met his specifications exactly!

It is also miraculous we met, because we live in different countries and we were right on the edge of the geographical limitations Tinder imposes. In fact the place I work is well outside those limitations and I was just spending a few days with my family.

The process is simple – write down what you want and then just say, out loud, "Universe, please give me ..."

My husband affirms that he has used this several times and there are some great books on the subject. just Google COSMIC ORDERING if you are interested.

Those of a religious disposition may prefer to ask their God, be it the three-headed elephant God of the Hindus, or the bearded old man of the Christians, it does not matter which, they all represent the same thing at the end of the day.

Number SIXTEEN
Work out practical marriage issues in advance

The title of this book is 100 Ways To Find A Husband, not 101 Ways To Get Laid. Many people have to base their ideas of married life on the way their parents organised things, because that's usually their only template. Attitudes will be greatly influenced on whether or not they had a happy childhood, if their parents had a stable relationship, or were around at all.

If your prospective husband is looking for a woman who will simply look after the house and be submissive, you better be damn sure that's the way you want it too. If you have a career of your own which brings in your own slice of income, and if you are emancipated and make your own decisions, then remember the male ego may not take kindly to getting (even more) shrivelled. Such issues need to be clearly resolved in advance. As do the questions of where you live, how you live and when you start.

As for the question of existing children and future children, this should bring you the most happiness and fulfilment, but it's vital you should decide what you want and make your decisions known as early in your relationship as possible.

Number SEVENTEEN
Keep your hairstyle stylish!

First impressions count. In my experience, it's a big mistake to make your hair too fancy, just as it is to ignore it. Your ideal husband will be marrying you, not your hair. Keep it natural, keep it clean, that's just common sense, and it's not just men who hate dirty, greasy hair, pretty much everyone does. When it comes to which areas of your body you shave and which you don't, that's showbiz.

Number Eighteen
Do not be afraid of an office romance

Letting opportunities pass you by is not the name of this game. In fact, many blissfully couples originally meet at work.

OK, it may not be ideal, and you may need to keep a low profile, but if something feels right then my advice to you is to go for it! You can bet on the fact that a boss rarely feels hindered by any such restriction and he or she would go for it with gusto if a suitable mate catches the eye.

Number Nineteen
Check out your wish list on a regular basis

Again I am not suggesting changing your criteria, but this is very different: your criteria does need reviewing every now and then.

Some women write down a list of what they want when they are in their teens and never change it. The real core of the problem is that the list usually has little to do with love and when that thunderbolt hits you may be surprised by the man who seems to have hurled it.

For example a lot of women go on about the "baggage" that a prospective husband carries, and that's fine …when you are in your teens! But a mature man would be a very sorry specimen if he did NOT have any baggage.

On top of that, if you insist on restricting your choice of potential life-partners to men with no baggage then you are cutting your chances of finding your husband by a huge percentage. Forget 1 in 5, it's more like 1 in 50. Some may say even 1 in 500.

So comb through your wish list regularly and hone it down to the absolute essentials. I tried to do exactly that and managed to reduce it to one line - we must both love each other!

That may sound trite but it covers all the bases, because ultimately you will not love anyone who does not meet your core values.

Number 20
Don't overdo the perfume

Come on girl, what exactly is it you're trying to cover up? Perfume is meant to be subtle, but some women throw it on like there's no tomorrow,

This can create a noxious cloud around us which will drive any man without a gas mask to run for the hills. Not a good idea. And nor do you want to add a strong smelling moisturizer or deodorant either.

When it comes to perfume, by all means go for the best you can afford, because the scent of a women is very important. But use it modestly, and that way it will not only have the desired effect, it'll save you money too.

Number 21
Develop a beautiful smile

A beautiful smile is a huge asset, so make sure you practice in front of the mirror. I'm not advising you to develop a fake grin, or a robotic reflex rictus, but to use your mirror to see what's in the eye of the man in your sights.

And avoid bright lip gloss. Woman to woman, I can assure you it detracts from the naturalness of your smile. And obviously you don't want yellow teeth and unhealthy breath.

Do this and you will keep your youth far longer than you might think possible. That is good for you, not just your mate!

Number 22
Don't play games (at least not too many)

When you find potential husband material you need to make yourself clear, and put yourself on the line a little. This is important.

Sure, sometimes it will backfire, but that's nowhere near as important as you may fear. What matters is letting a man who you like, and who think you may have a future with, become aware that you like him so that he knows you want him to stay in touch.

Of course he may not do that, but don't worry. Be true to yourself and don't play games. Just tell him how you feel. And if he does back off, there's always another great guy just round the corner.

As the woman said: "Next!"

Number 23
Focus

Once you find someone you like then focus, focus, focus on him.

It may be fun to play the field, but you risk losing something valuable. Ultimately such decisions are entirely up to you, and if you're not ready for a serious relationship then that's clearly an important factor, as long as you are honest with yourself.

But you might spend years regretting it if you lose someone with the potential for making an ideal husband just for the sake of a short term thrill.

Number 24
Everything matters

Men after a cheap thrill might appreciate pictures of you semi-naked or totally in the raw, but it's unlikely to appeal to a man who is seriously minded.

If you send explicit photos to one man they why wouldn't he assume you would send them to anyone who asks.

In these days of social media you have to be careful of the image you present.

Everything matters – but the “right” man is unlikely to hold your past against you unless you convince him it is also the present.

Number 25
Respect yourself

Don’t settle for less than the best! A mean man, whether financially or in his attitude to you, is not likely to become generous in the future.

Having said that, it has to work both ways and you too need to be reasonable. It's no good demanding diamonds and pearls when the guy can barely afford to keep body and soul together.

This is all about how you treat one another and respect one another, as well as how you respect yourself.

Number 26
Eye contact

Eye contact is a good way to start talking.

But don't be put off if the guy is looking back and meeting your gaze but not coming over. Some men are just so shy! The problem with being shy is that a shy person thinks that he will tend to make an initial bad impression, and that reinforces the whole problem.

I know this because my husband is very shy. OK, we met on Tinder so it was not an issue. But with some guys you need to make the move and go and talk to them.

(My friend's first wife did just that and they were married for 17 years!)

Number 27
Be very careful not to appear to be a gold digger (especially if you are!)

Men hate to feel they are being used, and my advice to you is to avoid giving this impression.

If you are in a social environment where people are having a drink, hold your drink in your hand, this way men can approach you without feeling they need to offer you a drink. In fact you can buy him a drink or whatever, occasionally. Men love that!

Don’t ask him what work he does too early in the conversation, or probe too fast on his financial status. Usually he'll volunteer this sort of information soon enough.

Number 28
Don’t panic!

Panic is the last thing you should ever do.

As I said right at the start, this is simply a numbers game and if you get out there, look your best, be alert, and work at it then you will succeed. In fact this works in all areas of life!

If you show signs of panic you will appear desperate, and you will never attract the right person into your life.

Number 29
Don’t be a perfectionist

Nobody is perfect, not even you, and it's pointless to look for perfection in a potential husband. Physically, morally or socially, finding an absolutely perfect husband is an unrealistic expectation.

Human life is not like that. You have to learn to take the rough with the smooth. My aim is to help your quest be a whole lot smoother than rougher!

Number 30
Don’t be afraid of failure

Too many of us women don't get out there and do stuff because of irrational fears, and our fear of failure is a major barrier to overcome.

Although this is more usually applied to business and the self-help industry it can be all-pervasive. If there is anything you don't do because of some fear, then that is an area of your life on which you may have slammed the door permanently. Please don't allow that, and make sure you get out there and do stuff!

There is a virtuous circle here:

- We try something new
- We fail BUT we learn
- We try something else new
- We fail but we learn more
- We try again and we SUCCEED (because we have learnt from out failures)

But the doomsday scenario is:

- We have an idea
- But we do nothing
- So we learn nothing
- So we NEVER succeed

One frightening statistic is that around 70% of people have little or no savings. But if these people, got out there and did stuff, and learnt new skills, they would succeed and get themselves out of this trap.

Failure is actually your friend and it bears many gifts, so get to know your friend and start to receive these gifts. Incidentally, schools bear a huge burden of guilt for not making this clear.

What has this got to do with finding your husband? Everything!

By following these guidelines you will be more successful, more able, and more positive, and all of these factors will help you find the right guy.

Failure is actually the best school in the world, it teaches far more than any other school possibly can!

Number 31
Ignore peer pressure

Another biggie here is the people around us.

Most people are not hugely successful, but we all have friends and family who we talk to and listen to. We take heed of these people and we hold them in great affection.

BUT what are their qualifications for guiding our life? What have they done with their lives?

I'm not saying they have not had good lives and I am not talking about paper qualifications, which in themselves have little meaning (it's what you do with them that counts).

I AM talking about whether they have travelled down the roads you want to go down yourself.

If they have, then they should be able to give you solid advice. But most people have not strayed far from the mainstream, they do not know what is on the other side, and so they tend to fear it.

On top of that, a lot of people are frightened of looking stupid and feel if they cannot answer a question that is how they may appear to you. So rather than say "I don't know anything about what you ask" they are liable to make up complete bullshit.

If you listen to it, you may be deterred from acting on a great idea which could have changed your life for the better.

If you want advice find people who have done what you want to do then talk to them!

Successful people generally love to help. The Universe has given them the opportunities for a good life (which they have grabbed with both hands) and they feel grateful.

Of course, this is not true of all successful people. But find people who have done what you want to do and they can be hugely useful to you.

Number 32
Don't be selfish

People who give are far more attractive than those who do not.

The more you give the more others accept you and want to be with you. This is probably one of the most obvious lessons we can learn, but many people are still selfish.

The more you think about other people, and ways to help them, the more attractive you become – another virtuous circle.

One obvious time to help is when a prospective husband has a problem.

Number 32
Don't talk too much about yourself

It's a huge mistake to dominate the conversation, and a fatal mistake to attempt to tell a man a complete potted history of your life, your loves, your achievements and your circumstances in as short a space of time as possible. You need to show an interest in your future husband, so ask him about himself.

Listening to someone else babble on about themselves can be very boring indeed. Conversation needs to flow. In particular don't just talk about the good stuff you are proud of, give a balanced view. By all means spice it up a bit, but talk about the stuff you are not so proud of as well, and invite a response.

Number 33
Listen

Listening is a very important skill.

Many people are so wrapped up in themselves they never listen properly. But there is nothing worse than having a conversation with somebody and then realising that the man in your sights has not been paying attention.

Number 34
Sex

It's impossible for me to give you clear guidelines on the multi-faceted topic of sex here, as there are so many factors in play.

However my instinctive advice is that it is generally better to delay full sex for a few dates as neither partner wants to think the other is "easy" or a slut.

We are talking about your future husband, and he may have views about marrying someone who seems happy to have a one-night stand.

For me, a good sequence has been…

- Date 1 – a goodnight peck
- Date 2 – a gentle snog
- Date 3 – a full-on snog
- Date 4 and onwards – eternal bliss!

That may seem old hat but it works, so why not try it!

Number 35
How often should you date this man?

I would recommend that you leave a few days between the initial dates.

If you made a good impression he will be looking forward to seeing you again, in fact he may think of nothing else!

So it's good to let those feelings percolate (yes, just like in your coffee machine) and mature.

This is not playing games, avoid that at all costs. No man worth having wants to be your plaything – at least not long term, an hour or two is something else of course!

Number 36
Develop winning habits

I mentioned earlier that 70% of people have little or no savings.

OK, that can make sense depending on where you are in your life and as long as you have some form of safety-net even if it is only available by means of additional credit on one or more credit cards.

But that cannot be described as a winning habit unless you are doing something constructive with the money, other than just funding an extravagant lifestyle. Something constructive might include funding a business idea or a project involving a potential new husband (of course).

However the concept of winning habits works across the board, in every aspect of your life.

We all have our own “distinctive character” but this does not mean we always get what we could get in every situation.

If you find you are not achieving your goals then you should work at developing those winning habits, but I am not saying it is easy.

Number 37
Female flesh

I'm sure I don’t need to tell you how appealing our flesh is to the opposite sex, and in some cases to the same sex.

But it can be “packaged” in many different ways and you may want to adapt the packaging depending on what sort of husband you want.

For example, successful and prosperous men (egomaniacal?) may want a woman who they can show off in society on a "look but don't touch" basis. Insecure men may want a wife they can show to their mother for approval. Shy men may be uncomfortable with a partner who reveals all, or they may relish bathing in the reflective glory.

So a more demure look may be the ticket, but that does not mean any less sexy!

Number 38
Look good, but sound good too

The right man will love you whatever you look and sound like, but if you want to increase the odds in your favour you may want to modulate how you sound.

Speaking at maximum volume is not a particularly attractive asset. Whispering or mumbling can be equally irritating. Cackling like a hyena is only attractive to other hyenas. Vocal tics, nervous coughs, dopey drivel and idiotic jargon will not help your cause at all. But if you have a particular accent or dialect there is nothing wrong with using it to your best advantage.

Recording yourself in conversation using your mobile phone is often a revelation, and I strongly advise you to do exactly this and learn from it.

Number 39
Smokes, drinks and recreational drugs

A significant percentage of people abhor smoking, and smoking is becoming more and more socially unacceptable. You will eliminate a significant percentage of eligible men from your target group if they know you smoke and they are dead set against the habit.

Obviously there are also health risks, which potential partners don't want to take, and there are also considerations about the health of any children you may have.

I'm not trying to be your nanny here, this is just how it is, and you know that anyway. Most men will refuse to kiss an ashtray unless they are an ashtray themselves. Having said that some men smoke too, and maybe smoking is something that may actually attract your perfect partner!

The same generality applies to alcohol too. If you are a boozer, then the chances of you finding a teetotal ideal husband are slim. If you happen to avoid alcohol for religious or health reasons then you will far better suited to a man who follows that same path that one who does not.

As for recreational drugs, you'll never discover the true personality of a man if he is addled, and he'll never discover yours either if you succumb.

In a book like this I am forced to generalise, and advice on smoking, alcohol and drugs each deserve a book to themselves! So I'll restrict my advice to being truthful to yourself about your own habits, and discover the truth about a prospective husband's habits as soon as you can.

Number 40
Be a doer, not a don'ter

There is a big difference!

When an opportunity comes along do you say “maybe” or do you go for it?

Well forget the maybe and get more positive. Start DOING, and don’t be a DON’TER!

(Thanks for the film *Pain Or Gain* for the inspiration.)

Number 41
Infinite love

The universe is made of love all you need to do is tap into that fact.

I should say at this point, and maybe I should have said this before, that not every one of these 101 suggestions is going to work for you, some will, of course, not even be relevant to you, for example you may smoke, you may not. You may have a liberated sexual appetite, you might be chaste.

However this suggestion gets right to the heart of the matter. Great philosophers and religious maniacs have been trying to figure out the universe ever since humans started to think, and they have not really made much real progress on the key issues. Why are we here? What are we meant to do here? What is the nature of death? What, if anything, happens after death.

Well, as far as I am concerned, the building block of the universe is love. Just look around you, see the wonderful world we live in and tap into that love!

There can be no real basis for finding a husband without it, and if the spark of love is not kindled then in my honest opinion you will fail in your relationship.

Number 42
Compete

It is a mitigating fact from our feminine perspective that the population of the world is 52% female. It means that we have to compete for our man from the 48% that is of the male persuasion.

Biologically this may make sense, in that women have the babies and for the survival of the species a greater number of women is important as we are vital.

We are, of course, more important than men is almost every way, but men still don’t seem to get this!

This fact underlies the need for this book. You need an edge. Get ready to compete.

Number 43
Dating agencies versus fee-based websites

If you don't like the internet and prefer the personal touch, there are still old-style dating agencies where you can go and chat through your requirements with an individual. Essentially it's a matchmaker service with a database.

They will not have as many people on their books as the online dating sites but the people they do have will be more serious and usually have some money – as these services can cost a fair bit more. There are fee-based operations that cost around $1000, but if you find the right person that seems a very small price to pay.

Number 44
Executive matchmakers

You can raise the stakes and pay a specialist $10,000 or more to match you to a high flyer.

Again in the scheme of things this is small priced to pay IF you find the right person, but I have never managed to find out what their success rate is. I would suggest asking before signing up, and then asking them to prove it!

Number 45
Be like me!

This will sound somewhat big-headed but I have had men falling over themselves to marry me.

To be clear, I used to have men falling over me until I met my wonderful husband. Is that better darling? (I get an unspecific humph in return).

So what's my secret?

We will be doing some private webinars on this, just email us at maryam@findahusband.info

Number 46
Be prepared to put some work in

Finding a husband is not like buying a car.

Relationships develop over time. When you first meet, you are looking at the raw material and you both need to work together to form the final product. When I met my wonderful husband we had an immediate problem, we did not speak the same language, literally so. He spoke English and I spoke French and Arabic. We also had quite significant cultural differences. We had to work through all this, and we still are, but it just gets better and better!

So you need to look into the future, get an idea of how the relationship might develop, and don't be ready to abandon ship if everything is not perfect on day one!

Number 47
Do a proper road test

Getting married is a big step.

In days long gone people had far less choice, and one of things they can now choose is to leave a marriage. In some ways this freedom is a good thing, but there are people with unrealistic expectations, maybe fostered by all the hyped advertising and celebrity culture we are exposed to, who might quickly walk away without putting in due effort.

This is not a good thing!

So we suggest you live together in the real world for a while to ensure, as far as possible, that it is going to work.

Number 48
Join a travel group

They say that a good test for a relationship is travelling together.

A lot of people find travel stressful, maybe you do too. By joining a group of single travellers you will see how they react to travelling, get to know them during the flight, ferry, train or coach journey.

You'll have easy conversation starters: where you are going to visit, how your day has been, where to go next, and conversation will flow from there.

Another advantage, especially if you are travelling abroad, is that you will have friends all over the world, which could create further travel possibilities.

Number 49
Go to a retreat

Retreats are great, you are brought together with complete strangers, and what better way to get to know people. But choose the type of retreat carefully, and understand that people's motivations for being there may be very different from your own.

Spiritual and self-growth seminars are very popular right now, and if you are looking for someone who may be out of the first bloom of youth this could be ideal.

Number 50
Learn something

Join a course. There are so many out there, and you will meet people in a relaxed atmosphere where you all have at least one connection – what you are learning.

Again be careful you choose something that you truly want to learn. Ideally this should be a passion!

Classes can develop skills you never knew you had, and allow you to meet a range of people doing the same. Amateur dramatics, language courses, music classes, whatever you have an aptitude for or an interest in. I tried a painting from life class, in the hope of judging the naked goods in advance of any date, but I soon switched to cake making.

There are also plenty of free sessions on FOREX trading and this might be a good place to meet investors who may be able to give you the life you dream of.

I am now giving my husband a chance to put forward the male point of view, the next 10 are his (there is some duplication here but from a different perspective).

Number 51
The Real Deal

Hi, good to speak to you!

My first point is an obvious one but, it used to crop up before I married Maryam. The point is that honesty and integrity are very important to me. OK, this is a personal statement but I think many guys will feel the same.

So if I turn up on a date and the woman looks nothing like the photo she showed me I am immediately on my guard – she has basically lied to me before we even met. I don't like liars!

If the reality was a significant improvement than the photo I would not be too bothered, I don't consider underselling a lie! But that has never happened, except that a photo is no match for the real thing!

Similarly if the woman is significantly older than she said. OK, I may shave off a few years myself but I treat the question "Age?" as an average. I am always being told I look 10 years younger than my age and my mental age remains in my teens! Of course, I'm male!

Pushing this too far is not only dishonest, it is also stupid, something else I most definitely do not want in a wife.

Number 52
Respect (and trust)

This is another big one!

I have been married before and I have children who I love very much. Plus I run my own business and that can seem very time consuming – although it also gives a lot of freedom.

I accept there are always issues when two people get together, but there has to be give and take and respect.

We all have some parts of our lives which are non-negotiable, and the real problem comes when two partners have such issues which are in conflict.

I'm a fairly thoughtful guy, my wife covered the different modalities earlier, our instincts, emotions and thoughts. Being thoughtful means I tend to think logically. Logically if two people love each other and trust each other than nothing else should really matter.

But instinctive and emotional people rarely care much for logic, and why should they? None of us is perfect, and we all know that, so trust is quite tough. But respect is essential! Actually I would say trust is also essential, it certainly makes everything much, much simpler.

Number 53
Arguments

Don't you just love 'em!

Many arguments are created by a lack of respect or trust, often fuelled by outside influences, at least that is my experience.

The problem with such situations is that people lose control and say things which can be hard to forgive. OK, I realise I am straying from "how to find a husband" into "how to keep a husband" – which is a subsequent book we are planning!

On the other hand, arguments prior to marriage may well mean there is never any marriage and thus no husband!

My main point is that arguments are usually avoidable and the ones that aren't can be handled better. I appreciate this is easier said than done and I have had some humdingers in my time (one time our flat was almost reduced to rubble!) but very few recently.

Number 54
The male/female divide

We each need different things and you have to build that into your relationship. I think we all know we are different. It is not Venus and Mars, but it does feel like it sometimes.

To me it is what makes a loving relationship so special but it can lead to problems if each party does not give the other sufficient consideration and space.

Men often complain that women change once they get their man, women complain that men won't change!!

We both need to get over this. We all change/mature over time and women need to stop hoping they can somehow fix a man.

Number 55
Money

Money is another area for potential conflict. First how we each feel about money is deeply personal and can vary a lot. My main business is trading financial markets and how a trader feels about money impacts his trades in all sorts of ways. The markets amplify the related emotions and instincts powerfully. We live in a consumer society, fuelled by unlimited and very sophisticated marketing – to a large extent we are consumer guinea pigs, what is all this marketing doing to us?

Many people seem to have self-esteem issues with money, unless they go shopping they feel they have no value. How absurd is this?

Our value lies in ourselves, not in what we may buy. Plus the more we spend now, the less we have in the future – no wonder so few people have any savings. I read in a wealth course I did recently that eliminating a modest consumption of alcohol plus around 10 cigarettes a day can built up to savings of around £250,000 over a 20 year period, if you take into account the investment returns on that money if saved.

Now I am no innocent when it comes to spending money and managed to develop a £100,000 financial black hole around 10 years ago. I was lucky, I pulled off a good business deal and cleared the lot in 12 months, but I always knew I had that opportunity and I worked hard to make it happen.

But, and it is a big BUT, the real issue here is that you do not ruin a perfectly good relationship because you both have very different views on money.

Number 56
TV

It is all too easy to fall into the habit of getting home form a tiring day at work plonking down in front of the TV and knocking back a few drinks or a tub of ice cream.

But this is not the way to a fulfilling life and you need to ensure that your quality of life is high.

It is all about you both being happy with the ways in which you live your life. It does not hurt to review how you both feel from time to time, and if there is scope for improvement then do some planning. There are so many ways in which people can improve their lives these days – just make sure you have a plan to get where you want to be!

Number 57
Quality time together

I don't need to say much on this point – just make sure you have plenty of good times together.

If you don't then it needs to be discussed.

You need to be prepared to make changes. Ultimately people ddon't usually waste time in a relationship with someone who doesn't value them.

Number 58
Children

Children may be very important to one or other partner, and hopefully with either both or neither. Clearly if one partner wants children but the other does not there is a clear mismatch.

It is important that such things be discussed as early and as clearly as possible.

Number 59
Confidence and Happiness

For my final point I want you to get away from the physical and into more important areas. What husbands really want is to be happy – actually this is what everybody wants!!

The most attractive people are those who exude confidence and happiness.

It should not really be so difficult – it is our natural state! But some of us seem to go the other way and end up exuding unhappiness and a lack of confidence.

Sadly these negatives impact hugely on the physical. I'm very lucky, my wife is a delight to be with!

That's all from me – back to Maryam

OK, I'm back and I hope you enjoyed my husband's comments. In the next section we are going to take a leaf out of the book *Seduction By The Stars* and look at those pesky star signs. By the way we strongly recommend this book. Actually my husband is helping me out here and we have a wealth of experience to offer…

Number 61
Aries

Aries, a fire sign, are the babies of the galaxy, and that is not necessarily a bad thing – it is very important to stay in touch with your inner child. Aries men identify with Tarzan, and so do Aries women! Sexual energy is raw and primeval. The book *Seduction by the Stars* suggests THE POUNCE! That speaks for itself!

Number 62
Taurus

The Bull, an earth sign, is a very different beast. Taurus men and women tend to be reliable and predictable unless you push them too far. Then you will wish you had not done so. Taurus loves food and they love nature, so combine those two and you are onto a winner.

Number 63
Gemini

The book sums up air sign Gemini as "I'm not schizophrenic – we're a Gemini!" They also tend to look like fairies, sprites, elves and, in the case of my husband's ex-wife's solicitor, like a goblin. In fact my husband reckons he can tell a Gemini just by looking at him or her. The books best advice is "If it were done when 'tis done, then 'twere well it were done quickly!" – meaning don't hang about!

Number 64
Cancer

Water sign Cancer may be the "nicest" sign of the galaxy and if you need nurturing this is the place. The key tactics are to get them to mother you and the seduction needs oodles of romance.

Number 65
Leo

Fire sign Leo (you had better believe it) is, of course, my husband's favourite!

Leo, the lion, likes the best of everything, so potential mates only have to convince them they are the best! Look out for the hair!

Number 66
Virgo

Earth sign Virgo strives to be healthy, wealthy and wise, pretty much in that order. They also tend to stay younger longer but can be seen as nit-picking. Virgos can be an acquired taste, but once acquired it can be hard to shake. The book suggests seduction by honesty!

Number 67
Libra

Air sign Libra rules partnerships and marriage. They are usually very stylish and user friendly. But they have to balance the emotional restraint of Virgo with the hot intensity of Scorpio. This a tough balancing act and it can make it hard for them to make decisions. The book *Seduction By The Stars* suggests SEDUCTION BY ASSUMPTION whereby you assume you will seduce your Libran and proceed accordingly; there is a fair chance by the time the Libran has reached a decision it may be too late!

Number 68
Scorpio

Ah Scorpio, and those of you who have had the "Scorpio" experience will understand just what I mean! Water sign Scorpio is not for the squeamish or the faint hearted!

A friend once had a huge fight with his Scorpio fiancée during which he tried to hold her down for his own safety. The Scorpio, in a voice straight out of The Exorcist, told him to let her go – thus giving me the most accurate confirmation ever that the book knows of what it talks. In the section "Scorpios at their worst" the book says "you will feel like a co-star in a real-life version of the Exorcist!"

It also recommends getting them to leave you if you ever need to part. Having said that I cannot help recommending the Scorpio experience – you certainly know you are alive!!

Number 69
Sagittarius

If you want to attract fire sign Sagittarius it is important to be positive. If, on the other hand, you want to get rid of one, simply develop a major depression or have a nervous breakdown.

Sagittarians like to do lots of stuff and they also like to do things their own way, so you need to be happy to go along.

They are also great seekers after truth. My husband's mother was a Sagittarian and he has inherited that from her. In fact both of his parent were fire signs, as am I, which might mean something!

Number 70
Capricorn

Earth sign Capricorn is associated with the goat, the horniest of beasts, and for good reason! But they can also offer emotional consistency, a sense of fair play, reliability, and a dry wit.

Of course all the good stuff can seem like the bad stuff to the wrong partner who is not too interested in their endless march up the hill of achievement.

Number 71
Aquarius

Air sign Aquarius is ruled by two very different planets - wild Uranus and practical Saturn. Ideally they will have the forces of these two planets in harmony. If not, the Uranus-dominated Aquarius may end up like a latter-day hippie. and the Saturn-dominated like a too-serious Capricorn without the benefits.

But the best ones will let you have all the space and time you need and you will have someone with whom you can share your wildest dreams, thoughts, theories, and passions!

Number 72
Pisces

Now we come to the final sign, the water sign Pisces who we might call the grand-daddy of the universe. Pisces is a fairly complex sign and the fish can take on many forms.

The book lists 4 in particular. Pisces Dropoutus, Pisces Misteriozus, Pisces Spongeoffus, and Pisces Superficialis, but there can be lots of good in this sign, and as the book says "You will feel you in a relationship with the most caring, sympathetic, accommodating person on the planet!"

That concludes our journey into the stars but it does not need to end here. We strongly recommend purchase of this book and find it incredibly useful, not just for seduction purposes (albeit that is now in the past) but also for insights into understanding any human relationship that may be causing difficulty. Just Google *Seduction By The Stars.- LINK NEEDED*

Number 73
Write a blog

One way of getting yourself out into the cyber world is to write about things that interest, concern, amuse, irritate, confuse or excite you about your life or the world at large.

People who have similar ideas or ideals to you could contact you and that could be an excellent starting point for a relationship.

Start by joining a web site like www.reddit.com and take your first steps.

Number 74
Speed dating

This is a great way to hone the first impression you make on people. You will only have two or three minutes with each person to do so, and it can seem rather hectic.

It has an advantage over dating websites, as you see the person in front of you, hear their voice and your first impression of them and your possible interest in them (or not) saves you hours of texting and phone calls before you meet them and then don't really connect.

You will want to practise your few minutes delivery, and remember that failing to plan is planning to fail!

We all have environments we prefer. If you have a great voice then a telephone call or audio presentation, as many dating sites use, may work well. We all have good photos of ourselves, at whatever age, but speed dating is a different kettle of fish. It may be daunting but certainly worth a try.

One good pointer – don't go into this hoping these people will like you – hope you will like them!

Number 75
Start a group

Depending on where you live there might be a wide choice of clubs or groups to join, or they might be few and far between. In either case you might spot a possibility for a group of your own and there will probably be people out there looking for the group you can create.

Any initiative of this type should be grabbed with both arms (and feet as well) as ideas like this have a magic to them – they can literally change your life.

All the great organisations and businesses in the world started with just such a thought – I want to do this! But so many give up between "I want to do this" and "I'm doing it!"

Don't be one of them, make the most of your life, go and get it done. You will have no shortage of potential husbands in the process!

Number 76
Go to exhibitions

As you wander around looking at paintings, ceramics, or whatever it is that is being exhibited you can casually start conversations with other people there.

They clearly have an interest in common with you, assuming they did not go there just to meet a partner. There again, maybe they are there for that reason as well!

Plus, as you wander around, you are exhibiting yourself in the way you choose to the kind of people your have already defined as being potentially right for you.

Number 77
Body language

Aside from eye contact, which some cultures struggle with, you should be aware of your general body language. Crossing your arms comes across as defensive and blocks the other person, whereas 'mirroring' someone indicates interest. If they lean forward, you lean forward, if they drink so do you, and so on.

This can get a little weird but I assure you it is also proven to be very effective.

Number 78
Volunteer

This is a great way to meet people who are like-minded, and there is a great call for volunteers for all sorts of things from beach clearing to soup kitchens, home and abroad.

You can be as adventurous or not, as you wish, and safe in the knowledge that whoever you meet is likely to be unselfish and altruistic.

You need to put the word out and a good site to start with is www.volunteerforever.com

But volunteering goes way beyond that. Simply offering to do stuff and help out generally is a great way of expanding your number of friends and of meeting people.

Number 79
People you meet have friends

Let's say you meet someone new but don’t connect with them romantically. Now consider that he has a friend who would be perfect for you.

Developing new friendship groups could be your gateway to love. So offer to help one other find the partner of your dreams.

Number 80
Start conversations

You can start a conversation with a simple "please" or "thank you", an observation of the weather, the season, or the time of day. In fact your opening gambit can be about anything. The point is you have to make it. Travelling on any form of transport, eating in the diner, having a sandwich on a park bench, you never know who you could be sitting next to.

So try chatting to them and see where the conversation goes.

Number 81
Don’t always judge a book by its cover

Although first impressions count, sometimes when you get to know a man better he can become more attractive to you. His personality may eclipse any reservations you may have had if his looks didn’t immediately grab you.

This is important as many men are hidden gems. If you don’t dig a little you will not find the gold and the diamonds below the surface.

Number 82
Host an event

It could be a garage sale, or a seminar in your field, or fund-raising for a local charity. Again you'll meet people who have a similar interest to you, or people who have a similar interest and friends they could introduce you to.

It might just be an excuse for a party!

Number 83
Get in touch with old friends (who have friends)

Obviously if the friendship ended badly this may not be the best idea, but in my experience people you drifted away from in the past can be a good way to expand your social group and meet new people.

Number 84
Step out of your comfort zone

This isn't the easiest option, but it can be incredibly rewarding. We all tend do develop habits in life including the habitual places we go. A definition of madness is, 'To continue to do the same thing and expect different results.' By going to different places you will meet different people and gain new experiences. If what you are doing now and where you are going aren't bringing you the results you want, then change them.

By the way, to take dangerous risks then "to continue to do the same thing and NOT expect different results" may not be madness, but it is dumb. So if you drive too fast too often you should expect to get stopped by the police, flashed by a speed camera, or be involved in an accident – over time that is pretty much inevitable!

Number 85
Trust your gut

This is a very undervalued and often ignored instinct. We all get 'feelings' about people. It could be that we don't trust them, or even like them, when all they have done is said 'Hello.' Trust those feelings because this is your subconscious at work, picking up on signals that we don't consciously register.

Of course, this does not necessarily help you find the "right" one, but it may well stop you wasting time on the wrong one!

Number 86
Confused?

Sometimes we find that people tell us one thing but seem to do something else. Or maybe their body language contradicts what they are saying.

Well there is one simple rule to help out. If you are confused by a man's contradictory words or deeds, remember actions always speak louder than words. So focus on what a man actually does, not what he says!

Number 87
Handling a relationship

There are a few points here…

1. Don't judge a new partner based on your experiences in the past. It is all too easy to bring your prejudices to a new relationship, and this can be fatal. Start afresh!

2. Conversely, don't put a partner on a pedestal, they may decide to look down on you!
3. Try not to make assumptions, if you are unsure then talk about it.
4. Don't invest more in the relationship than your partner, albeit there need to be exceptions from time to time.
5. Don't get too carried away with the future until you have built the bedrock of the relationship in the present.
6. Dates are a learning experience, be open and be present. Learn as much as you can about the man you meet, learn more about dating, and have fun!
7. Think about the sort of man you want. If you like a guy who takes charge then don't compete with him!

Number 88
Self-Esteem

This is a big one, hence number 88, the luckiest number between 1 and 101, at least according to the Chinese.

Self-esteem governs us in many, many ways and it is said that the quality of the man we attract is equal to our self-esteem. I believe this is true because it is our self esteem which can turbo-charge our attractiveness.

This problem is that it can be hard to raise your self esteem, especially if life has whacked you a few times. But it is something you really need to do if low self esteem is an issue.

There are plenty of books on this matter and also courses you can attend. If you want any help with this get in touch and we will see what we can put together. Never accept any obstacles, they can all be broken down given will, perseverance, and planning! Never forget that!

Number 89
His age

This is in two parts because I believe there are two distinct aspects to age. The first is the age of the partner you are looking for.

It is traditional wisdom that men mature more slowly than women, although as with all such things there are many exceptions, some startling. But in the earlier years, women usually have the advantage and men do the chasing. This gives women two advantages, first they are generally more mature and therefore can have more control, secondly men want what they have. However as the years roll by, men catch up, become more mature and self assured and maybe acquire some material assets. At this point the balance of power can swing. It is actually up to the individual, no one needs to give up control.

In the early years, a woman can pretty much have any man she wants. But this gets more difficult as the years pass, especially once a woman can no longer have children.

I think it is impossible to give guidelines on the age of the partner you should look for, other than to say that the younger you want the more you will restrict the availability. Having said, that I know many happy couples with widely disparate age gaps, albeit in the main the men tend to be older than the women, or at least of similar ages. I do not know many couples where the woman is significantly older than the man, but I do know they exist.

This brings me to the next age factor.

Number 90
Your age

Numeric age, meaning based on your date of birth, is not hugely significant because there are various factors that determine what we will call "true" age. Some of these are:

1. Your date of birth – there is no getting away from that.
2. Your mental age – men generally have the advantage here (as many older men still think like teenagers – is this an advantage? - discuss!)
3. How you look after your self physically.
4. How you look after yourself mentally – use it or lose it!
5. How much you abuse yourself, alcohol, cigarettes, etc, but even environment is a factor, such as living in polluted cities.
6. Your life-style generally.
7. How happy you are – this is very important.
8. Your self-esteem (obviously).

I could go on forever, but what I am calling "true" age can differ from the time you have actually spent on this planet, and it can vary in both the older or younger direction.

It is "true" age that counts and, of course, you can take action to change your "true" age, but it does take time!

Number 91
Give him a chance

Some men may take time to grown on you. I would suggest giving the ones where there is potential a second or third chance.

This may not be your normal approach. All I can say is I almost did not see my husband a second time, and that would have been a big mistake!!

Number 92
Perseverance (1)

This also comes in two parts and is another essential factor.

Unless you persevere, you never achieve anything worthwhile in life. OK, sure, a few things will fall into your lap, but this is the exception. If you want something, then you need to work at it and this is as true in life generally as it is in relationships.

I never said relationships were easy, and if I did I was wrong! In fact nothing worthwhile is easy, so if you are prone to throw in the towel fairly quickly you will just live your life like a pinball in a pinball machine, forever bouncing to and fro before you disappear down that big black hole!

So fight for what you want and persevere. This does not mean flogging a dead horse, but do not give up on a good thing for trivial reasons.

Number 93
Perseverance (2)

This applies both in a relationship (critically so) but also in the dating process.

Not only should you not give up the dating process, despite however many setbacks, but you should also not give up with any one particular frog just because he is taking longer than you might hope to turn into a prince.

You may be talking about the rest of your life here, so a little extra effort is worthwhile. But you want to see effort from the other side too. It can be a mistake for you to invest more in the relationship than he is.

Number 94
Stubbornness

We all have stubborn streaks and we are entitled to them.

However you don't want to let that ruin your life, and you might just do that if one or other of you start behaving liked a mule. This can jeopardise a relationship that might just work long term, but because of stubbornness you will never let it happen.

There is stubborn and there is a word that sounds like mule but begins with F!

Number 95
Laziness

Then there is laziness. You get the most out of life if you give a lot. The more you give, the more you get!

Laziness rather limits your capacity to do very much at all and you certainly won't be giving too often. Of course we all have our lazy moments, but if laziness dominates your life you will never put in the effort to find your ideal husband.

Number 96
In the morning

In your quest for a husband I recommend seeing any prospect when they wake up in the morning.

How you achieve this is up to you. But one word of warning, if you do find the ONE it may be better for your wedding plans to not see him when he wakes up too early in the relationship!

Number 97
Be Natural

In a relationship it is important to be yourself.

Sure, put on a front to land your man but show the real you as well. There is no point being in a relationship where you have to pretend all the time. Plus, of course, true commitment can only be between two real people, if one is pretending it will not work. Your natural self is who your future husband will be marrying, not a construct or an act.

Number 98
Fighting

When two people are in love they don't want to hurt each other. But fuelled by emotion, with added alcohol, or stress, or debt, or falsehoods, or whatever, it happens.

Believe me, it is much better to find an acceptable solution without the argument. Remember when you find the ONE his happiness and yours are one and the same!

Number 99
Awaken the inner goddess

You know she is in there, so let her loose and let her attract your soul mate

OK, this is easier said than done. We are all so busy letting our egos have their way and worrying about all the stuff that does not really matter. But what has all that worrying ever done for you? You are still here, aren't you, and if you had not spent all that time worrying you could have been doing far more constructive things.

Awaken your inner goddess, no matter how deep she is hiding, and let her lead you.

Number 100
If all else fails, pray!

I told you about cosmic ordering earlier, and prayer is similar but not quite the same.

Ask others to pray with you and for you, and don't be ashamed or shy to do so. This may seem extreme but we are at number 100! Anyway, I am telling you that there is power in asking the universe for what you want, and that power is increased the more people who are involved.

Be clear, be specific, believe truly that you deserve the best, the most gentle, the most loving and caring man!

Stake your claim my sisters, and succeed in your quest.

Number 101
Throw away your list and start again

OK, I said I would not mess with your criteria, but if all else fails you have no choice. In any case, your list may be totally wrong. You don’t really know who will make you truly happy until you find him, so if all else fails just throw away your list, look carefully around you, and start over.

Take a deep breath, relax, you are still alive, you have plenty of time!

Good luck, and don't forget to send me your wedding invitation.

101 WAYS TO FIND A HUSBAND

Ask, tell, share.

maryam@findahusband.info

www.findahusband.info

Printed in Great Britain
by Amazon